Heart to Heart

17 Favorite Songs and Hymns of Worship

Arranged for Solo Piano by Roger House

Contents

Lillenas PUBLISHING COMPANY

KANSAS CITY, MO 64141

Give Thanks

HENRY SMITH
Arr. by Roger House

Moderately

4

Happily

Adoration Medley
He Is Lord
We Worship and Adore You

Arr. by Roger House

Tenderly, slowly

"He Is Lord" (Unknown)

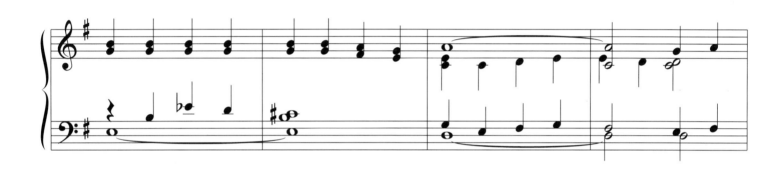

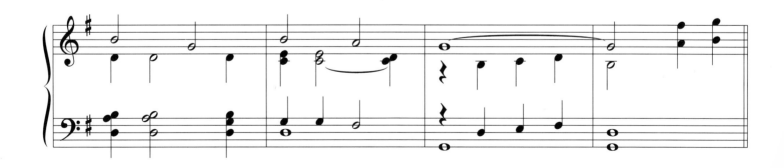

"We Worship and Adore You" (Traditional)

8

When I Look into Your Holiness

WAYNE & CATHY PERRIN
Arr. by Roger House

13

Blessed Assurance

PHOEBE P. KNAPP
Arr. by Roger House

Confidently

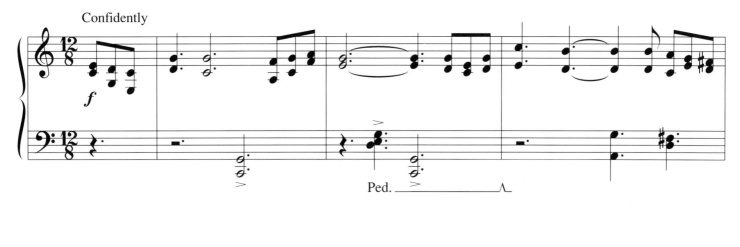

16

I Will Sing of the Mercies

JAMES H. FILLMORE
Arr. by Roger House

It Is Well with My Soul

PHILIP P. BLISS
Arr. by Roger House

Moment by Moment

MAY WHITTLE MOODY
Arr. by Roger House

Slowly

A little faster

mf

Slower

rubato

29

Praise to the Lord, the Almighty

From *Stralsund Gesangbuch*
Arr. by Roger House

Evenly, not too fast

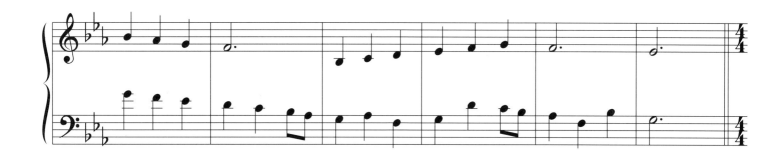

To God Be the Glory

WILLIAM H. DOANE
Arr. by Roger House

35

Softly and Tenderly

WILL L. THOMPSON
Arr. by Roger House

Tenderly, with feeling

11-3-97 amo

Name of Jesus Medley

Oh, How I Love Jesus
Jesus Is the Sweetest Name I Know
Take the Name of Jesus with You

Arr. by Roger House

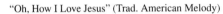

"Oh, How I Love Jesus" (Trad. American Melody)

"Jesus Is the Sweetest Name I Know" (Lela Long)

Slower

"Take the Name of Jesus with You" (William H. Doane)

All Hail the Power of Jesus' Name

Arr. by Roger House

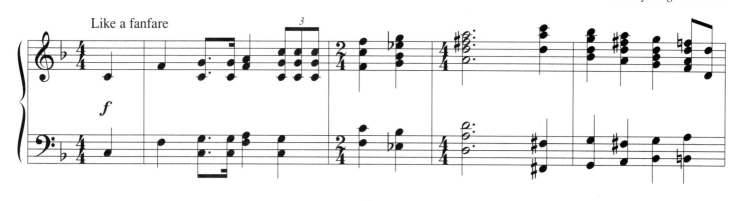

TUNE: Diadem (James Ellor)

TUNE: Coronation (Oliver Holden)

A bit slower, grandly

slight rit.

And Can It Be?

THOMAS CAMPBELL
Arr. by Roger House

I Am Thine, O Lord

WILLIAM H. DOANE
Arr. by Roger House

With freedom

More delicate

rubato

a tempo

rubato

Slower